Film Chinois

by

Damon Chua

NEW YORK HOLLYWOOD LONDON TORONTO

SAMUELFRENCH.COM

Copyright © 2008 by Damon Chua

ALL RIGHTS RESERVED

CAUTION: Professionals and amateurs are hereby warned that *FILM CHINOIS* is subject to a royalty. It is fully protected under the copyright laws of the United States of America, the British Commonwealth, including Canada, and all other countries of the Copyright Union. All rights, including professional, amateur, motion picture, recitation, lecturing, public reading, radio broadcasting, television and the rights of translation into foreign languages are strictly reserved. In its present form the play is dedicated to the reading public only.

The amateur live stage performance rights to *FILM CHINOIS* are controlled exclusively by Samuel French, Inc., and royalty arrangements and licenses must be secured well in advance of presentation. PLEASE NOTE that amateur royalty fees are set upon application in accordance with your producing circumstances. When applying for a royalty quotation and license please give us the number of performances intended, dates of production, your seating capacity and admission fee. Royalties are payable one week before the opening performance of the play to Samuel French, Inc., at 45 W. 25th Street, New York, NY 10010.

Royalty of the required amount must be paid whether the play is presented for charity or gain and whether or not admission is charged.

Stock royalty quoted upon application to Samuel French, Inc.

For all other rights than those stipulated above, apply to: Grove Theater Center, P.O. Box 2090 Long Beach, CA 90801. Att: Charles Johanson.

Particular emphasis is laid on the question of amateur or professional readings, permission and terms for which must be secured in writing from Samuel French, Inc.

Copying from this book in whole or in part is strictly forbidden by law, and the right of performance is not transferable.

Whenever the play is produced the following notice must appear on all programs, printing and advertising for the play: "Produced by special arrangement with Samuel French, Inc."

Due authorship credit must be given on all programs, printing and advertising for the play.

ISBN 978-0-573-66330-7   Printed in U.S.A.   #8959

No one shall commit or authorize any act or omission by which the copyright of, or the right to copyright, this play may be impaired.

No one shall make any changes in this play for the purpose of production.

Publication of this play does not imply availability for performance. Both amateurs and professionals considering a production are strongly advised in their own interests to apply to Samuel French, Inc., for written permission before starting rehearsals, advertising, or booking a theatre.

No part of this book may be reproduced, stored in a retrieval system, or transmitted in any form, by any means, now known or yet to be invented, including mechanical, electronic, photocopying, recording, videotaping, or otherwise, without the prior written permission of the publisher.

IMPORTANT BILLING AND CREDIT REQUIREMENTS

All producers of *FILM CHINOIS* must give credit to the Author of the Play in all programs distributed in connection with performances of the Play, and in all instances in which the title of the Play appears for the purposes of advertising, publicizing or otherwise exploiting the Play and/or a production. The name of the Author *must* appear on a separate line on which no other name appears, immediately following the title and *must* appear in size of type not less than fifty percent of the size of the title type.

In addition, all producers of *FILM CHINOIS* must give credit to the original producers of the play in all programs. This billing is to appear at the bottom of the title page in type equal or larger than the smallest name on the piece and at no time less than equivalent in size to 7 point Times Roman and on a separate line from any other information. The credit will appear as follows:

"*FILM CHINOIS* premiered at Grove Theater Center in Burbank, California. Kevin Cochran, Artistic Director. Charles Johanson, Executive Director.".

Opening Night: 7 July 2007 at GTC Burbank

Real. Live. Fun.

Grove Theater Center

Kevin Cochran, Artistic Director
Charles L Johanson, Executive Director

film chinois

written by	**Damon Chua**
directed by	**Kevin Cochran**

Cast (in order of appearance)

Chinadoll	**Elizabeth Pan**
Randolph	**Sean Dougherty**
The Man	**Sam Mak**
Simone	**Joyce F. Liu**
Ambassador	**Frank Simons**
Lights	**David Darwin**
Set & Costumes	**Leonard Ogden**
Sound	**Hunter Stephenson**
Projections	**Walter Lutz**

Film Chinois was developed through the GTC New Play Initiative (www.gtc.org).

Literary Manager	**Sondi Kroeger Foley**
Primary Reader	**Ruth Seigle**

Produced for Grove Theater Center by Kevin Cochran & Charles Johanson

CHARACTERS

CHINADOLL - Early thirties, a Maoist/communist spy. She is the Chinese equivalent of the classic femme fatale.

RANDOLPH - Early thirties, an American operative. Smart, cool and collected, but in many ways, an innocent abroad.

SIMONE - Twenties, a Chinese songstress with a few tricks up her sleeve. Willful, emotional and a little silly.

AMBASSADOR - Fifties or older, from Belgium. Seedy, amoral and dryly funny, he is a steadfast admirer of Asian women.

THE MAN, who plays:

    WAITER (Scenes 1 & 13)

    CHINESE BUSINESSMAN (Scenes 2 & 16)

    SERVER (Scene 3)

    CHINESE MAN (Scenes 7, 11 & 15)

    HOTEL CLERK (Scene 14)

    WOMAN (Scene 17)

AUTHOR'S NOTE

A silent, black-and-white short film is required for the last scene of the play. In the absence of such a film, the effect may be suggested by a flickering square of dim white light.

Scene One: Restaurant

(A dimly lit space with a sense of after-hours lethargy. **CHINADOLL**, *smoking, nursing a coffee, watches in cool contemplation the smoke curling up into the darkness of the ceiling.*

She composes herself and faces the audience.)

CHINADOLL. The year, 1947. The city, Beijing. Location, a quiet restaurant in the Diplomatic District. A beautiful girl sits smoking and drinking coffee. It is late. The beautiful girl is tired from a hard day's work looking for a film. As her thoughts turn to sleep, a stranger walks in.

(RANDOLPH *enters.)*

CHINADOLL. Her thoughts change, quickly.

(Immediately noticing the beautiful girl, **RANDOLPH** *takes a seat at the table next to hers.* **WAITER** *enters, gives him a menu, and exits.)*

CHINADOLL. There are stories of coincidences. Amazing tales of luck. But nothing like this. This is fate. The beautiful girl, still tired, knows exactly what she must do. Out of the corner of her eyes, she takes in the man's every move. She knows that if she does her job well, she will be free. Then, suddenly, his voice.

RANDOLPH. I was wondering…

CHINADOLL. The beautiful girl's heart skips a beat. No, she isn't attracted to him. Not yet. That comes later. Now she has to sustain his interest. In an indirect way. Which is, as she knows, the only way.

RANDOLPH. I was wondering…if you had a light.

*(***CHINADOLL** *pulls out a lighter.* **RANDOLPH** *goes up to her with a cigarette. She lights it.)*

RANDOLPH. Thank you. *(Beat)* What is your name?

CHINADOLL. It isn't the hardest of questions. And the beautiful girl has several answers. It depends on who's asking. For now, she says: *Chinadoll.*

RANDOLPH. Chinadoll. What a pretty name.

CHINADOLL. When a man says 'what a pretty name,' it may be difficult to know what he means. It could be, simply, I find you pretty. Or it could be, I find you repulsive, only your name is pretty. To know the truth, one has to listen carefully. Was it…

RANDOLPH. What a pretty *name.*

CHINADOLL. In which case it's only the name that appeals. Or was it…

RANDOLPH. What a *pretty* name.

CHINADOLL. In which case there is hope. I would like to think he meant the latter.

RANDOLPH. What a *pretty* name.

CHINADOLL. I've been called pretty all my life. But I prefer 'beautiful.' At the age of three, my Uncle's neighbor, an old man with large Buddha ears, called me a pretty little Princess. At the age of eight, I blushed when a cousin visiting from *Wuhan* called me pretty to my face. But by the time I was ten, I knew how to deal with 'pretty.' I would say, to the hordes of pre-pubescent boys with bad teeth and bad breath, 'and what do you have in mind?' They would cower and run away, almost surprised that a girl would come up with such a remark. So the beautiful girl almost said: *And what do you have in mind?*

RANDOLPH. Well…

(Beat.)

CHINADOLL. It works for boys. But not for men who know a thing or two about women. So, I say nothing.

RANDOLPH. My name is Randolph. I'm from America.

CHINADOLL. But she knows that already. Randolph Edward Dean, aged thirty-two, born and raised in Nebraska, educated at Yale, working for the U.S. Government in an undefined capacity.

RANDOLPH. I'm a tea trader.

CHINADOLL. That's what they all say. Tea trader. So she says: *How's the tea harvest this season?*

RANDOLPH. Good. Very good.

CHINADOLL. The conversation is going nowhere. She knows she doesn't have much time. She tries: *How do you like Beijing, or Peking, as you people call it?*

RANDOLPH. I'm liking it more and more each day.

CHINADOLL. That was weak; she has to try harder. So the beautiful girl asks him a question to which answer she already knows: *What do you think of that rebel Mao Tse-Tung? He's been in the news a lot lately.*

RANDOLPH. That's a question of some delicacy.

CHINADOLL. He knows how to spin it.

RANDOLPH. He's striking a chord with the masses out there – the peasants and farmers who are the backbone of this country. Support is growing. What do you think?

CHINADOLL. He knows his stuff. The beautiful girl decides to play along: *That's exactly the problem – appealing to the masses and leaving the intellectuals behind. It's tearing the country apart.*

RANDOLPH. Perhaps it's for the better. Change is not always a bad thing.

CHINADOLL. Which was not what he said. At a meeting in Baltimore. A secret meeting. Just a month before.

RANDOLPH. But why talk about Mao when we can talk about the beauty of Peking. Or Beijing, as you people call it.

CHINADOLL. That was a nice segue. I have to give it to him. *You find Beijing beautiful do you?*

RANDOLPH. Very much so.

CHINADOLL. More beautiful than America?

RANDOLPH. In many ways.

CHINADOLL. More beautiful than your wife? *(Beat)* No, she didn't actually say that, even though the words were at the tip of her tongue. Now they are on firmer ground. She says: *If you're looking for something authentically Chinese, this is not the restaurant. Perhaps you'd like me to take you somewhere, somewhere that will set your taste buds on fire.*

*(**RANDOLPH** is almost at a loss for words.)*

RANDOLPH. I'm game.

*(**CHINADOLL** finally meets his eyes.)*

CHINADOLL. Shall we?

*(**RANDOLPH** stands up.)*

CHINADOLL. It works every time. But that's just the start. And there are many steps in this mysterious process. The beautiful girl sets aside her fatigue and mentally prepares herself for what is to come. She has a deadline after all. And things, as the future Chairman Mao would say, will only get more interesting.

*(**CHINADOLL** stands up and extends her beautiful hand, as lights fade.)*

End of Scene

Scene Two: Nightclub

(A lone spot on a beautifully-clad **SIMONE**, *on stage, singing a Zhou Xuan song.*

As lights go up, we see **AMBASSADOR**, *sitting at a table near the stage, nursing a cognac. He is lost in Simone's voice.*

CHINESE BUSINESSMAN *enters, tentative, carrying a briefcase. He is dressed in an ill-fitting suit.*

The following action takes place over the song.

CHINESE BUSINESSMAN *scans the room and spots* **AMBASSADOR**. *He moves towards an adjacent table.*

AMBASSADOR *does not acknowledge Chinese Businessman. Instead, after a beat, he stands up and moves to exit. Along the way he very discreetly drops a small but bulky envelope onto Chinese Businessman's table.* **AMBASSADOR** *exits.*

CHINESE BUSINESSMAN *quickly picks up the envelope and looks into it. It is stuffed full of cash. It is only then that* **CHINESE BUSINESSMAN** *smiles.*

He opens his briefcase, takes out a larger envelope containing something. This he leaves on the table. After a beat, **CHINESE BUSINESSMAN** *picks up his briefcase and exits.*

Momentarily **AMBASSADOR** *re-enters, waving to the still-singing* **SIMONE** *who flirts back in acknowledgement.* **AMBASSADOR** *spots the larger envelope and picks it up discreetly on the way back to his table.*

As he sits, he opens up the envelope, revealing a CAN OF FILM. Just then Simone's song draws to a close. **AMBASSADOR** *claps, as* **SIMONE** *blows him a kiss, making her way to the exit.)*

AMBASSADOR. Leaving so soon?

SIMONE. Mister Ambassador.

AMBASSADOR. *Mon petit pois.* Won't you come join me for a while?

(**SIMONE** *weighs her options, and goes to sit with her suitor.*)

AMBASSADOR. I love your singing.

SIMONE. You say that every time.

AMBASSADOR. Because you're good. Always.

SIMONE. *(Not meaning it)* You're too kind.

AMBASSADOR. So what is my little chanteuse up to these days?

SIMONE. You know what I do.

AMBASSADOR. *(Mock surprise)* Do I really?

(**AMBASSADOR** *takes a good look at* **SIMONE**.)

AMBASSADOR. Want a little drink? I'm buying.

SIMONE. Any news of my transit papers?

AMBASSADOR. Ah, the transit papers. Alas, I have no news. No news at all.

SIMONE. I'm tired of this game.

AMBASSADOR. Game? You think this is a game?

SIMONE. I can't do this much longer.

AMBASSADOR. What do you suggest?

(**SIMONE** *has no response.* **AMBASSADOR** *laughs.*)

AMBASSADOR. You see. You need me. And I need you.

SIMONE. I'm really tired.

AMBASSADOR. Poor little baby. So tired. So uncooperative.

SIMONE. I saw the man with the briefcase. Maybe he likes you. Maybe you can try him.

(**AMBASSADOR**'s *smile vanishes.*)

AMBASSADOR. Watch what you say.

SIMONE. Whatever *thing* he gets you, I can get it too.

AMBASSADOR. Thanks but no thanks.

SIMONE. Just tell me what you want.

AMBASSADOR. You know what I want. *(Beat)* So?

SIMONE. What about tomorrow?

AMBASSADOR. I'm busy.

SIMONE. The day after then.

AMBASSADOR. No. It's tonight or nothing.

SIMONE. I need to do something first.

AMBASSADOR. I'm not falling for that.

SIMONE. Ambassador.

AMBASSADOR. I give you one hour. You know where I live.

SIMONE. You're hateful.

   (**AMBASSADOR** *smiles.*)

SIMONE. Give me a cigarette.

   (**AMBASSADOR** *does so, and lights it.*)

AMBASSADOR. By the way, have you heard of "The Twins?"

SIMONE. The Twins?

AMBASSADOR. Chinese. Maoists. Operate around Peking.

SIMONE. No. Why?

AMBASSADOR. No reason.

SIMONE. Why are you interested in them?

AMBASSADOR. I'm always interested in 'them.'

SIMONE. I'm a Maoist too.

AMBASSADOR. You?

SIMONE. Why not? I think I'd look really good in a Mao suit.

AMBASSADOR. Maybe so. But you're like me, a true capitalist.

   (**AMBASSADOR** *takes out a wad of cash from his jacket.*)

AMBASSADOR. Right?

   (**SIMONE** *tries to take the cash, but the* **AMBASSADOR** *moves it away quickly.* **SIMONE** *laughs, despite herself.*)

SIMONE. You know why I like you?

AMBASSADOR. *(Mocking)* You like me?

SIMONE. Stop it.

AMBASSADOR. Tell me why you like me.

SIMONE. Because, well, you do what you want, say what you like.

AMBASSADOR. And you like that?

SIMONE. Sure.

AMBASSADOR. That's what you see in me? I thought I'm just your, how-do-you-say, meal ticket.

SIMONE. That too.

AMBASSADOR. How easily I fall for your sweet lies.

SIMONE. But you like it.

AMBASSADOR. I'm just humoring you.

SIMONE. You're making fun of me.

AMBASSADOR. What else is there to do? For me it's just wine, woman and song.

SIMONE. You're the Ambassador.

AMBASSADOR. Of a small, unimportant country.

SIMONE. Belgium is not small. Right?

AMBASSADOR. Wrong. It's tiny.

SIMONE. But it's beautiful. I know it's beautiful.

AMBASSADOR. Perhaps so.

SIMONE. It would be nice to live there.

AMBASSADOR. We shall see.

SIMONE. Europe – the center of the world. The culture, the cities, sophisticated people, where the air is fresh and food is good…

AMBASSADOR. Enough of this chit-chat.

*(***SIMONE*** looks annoyed.*

AMBASSADOR *takes a bill from the wad of cash and gives it to* **SIMONE**.*)*

AMBASSADOR. I give you one hour.

*(***SIMONE*** smiles, slips the cash into her dress, as lights fade.*

End of Scene

Scene Three: Imperial Palace Gardens

(Evening. Sounds of a Chinese orchestra playing.

Lights up on **RANDOLPH**, *standing in an outdoor pavilion, being served drinks by* **SERVER**. *As* **SERVER** *exits,* **CHINADOLL** *enters.*

There is a beat as **RANDOLPH** *registers the beautiful girl before his eyes.)*

RANDOLPH. Can this be real?

(**CHINADOLL** *contemplates the question.*)

CHINADOLL. There is a Chinese saying. A fly never visits an egg that is not cracked.

RANDOLPH. You look more beautiful than ever.

CHINADOLL. You're not interested in what I have to say.

RANDOLPH. Hi.

CHINADOLL. What brings you to the Imperial Palace Gardens?

RANDOLPH. I wanted to ask you the same.

CHINADOLL. I asked first.

RANDOLPH. It's obvious, isn't it? Look at this place. It is like heaven on earth.

CHINADOLL. It used to be more beautiful. Before the war.

RANDOLPH. The war.

(Beat.)

CHINADOLL. You didn't answer my question.

RANDOLPH. I was invited.

CHINADOLL. You came alone?

RANDOLPH. I chose to come alone. And you?

CHINADOLL. I was invited too.

RANDOLPH. We're both invited.

CHINADOLL. How nice.

RANDOLPH. I have been thinking. About you.

CHINADOLL. Have you?

RANDOLPH. Yes.

CHINADOLL. What have you been thinking?

RANDOLPH. That our meeting at the restaurant wasn't an accident.

CHINADOLL. Is that what you think?

RANDOLPH. Yes.

CHINADOLL. Why?

RANDOLPH. Call it intuition.

CHINADOLL. I wasn't there to meet anyone.

RANDOLPH. I didn't say you were.

CHINADOLL. You spoke to me first.

RANDOLPH. It was quite courageous of me, don't you think?

CHINADOLL. Not really.

RANDOLPH. When in a public place a man speaks to a woman whom he doesn't know…

CHINADOLL. That is not courage. That's foolishness.

RANDOLPH. Then I'm glad I was a fool.

(The Chinese orchestra strikes up again, this time playing "In a Sentimental Mood.")

RANDOLPH. Would you like to dance?

CHINADOLL. I'd rather not.

RANDOLPH. Can I not persuade you?

CHINADOLL. You can try.

RANDOLPH. I'd really like to.

CHINADOLL. I have a confession to make.

*(**RANDOLPH** contemplates this peculiar remark.)*

RANDOLPH. A confession.

CHINADOLL. Well… I…

(Beat.)

RANDOLPH. What is it?

CHINADOLL. I cannot dance.

RANDOLPH. That makes two of us. Please?

(**CHINADOLL** *concedes. They move towards each other, tentative, but once they start engaging with the rhythm, it's like they've been dancing together all their lives.*)

RANDOLPH. Did you grow up here?

CHINADOLL. Nobody grows up in Beijing. I was born in a village in *Hubei*. Didn't see a city till I turned twenty.

RANDOLPH. I grew up in a small town too. Have you heard of Franklin, Nebraska?

CHINADOLL. No.

RANDOLPH. It's right in the middle of the country.

CHINADOLL. Do you miss it?

RANDOLPH. Do I miss home?

CHINADOLL. Yes.

RANDOLPH. Sometimes. Do you?

CHINADOLL. Beijing is my home now.

RANDOLPH. Your family?

CHINADOLL. They are all dead.

RANDOLPH. I'm sorry.

CHINADOLL. They died during the war.

RANDOLPH. I'm really sorry.

CHINADOLL. I like being by myself, to tell the truth.

RANDOLPH. You're not alone anymore.

CHINADOLL. We're just dancing.

RANDOLPH. Enjoying yourself?

CHINADOLL. What you want me to say?

RANDOLPH. Say yes.

(**CHINADOLL** *stops, pulls away even as the orchestra continues to play.* **RANDOLPH**, *unhappy, follows her.*)

CHINADOLL. Who do you think are the people who come to this party?

(**RANDOLPH** *surveys the crowd.*)

RANDOLPH. What do you think?

CHINADOLL. I think all of them have a little secret in them.

RANDOLPH. Is that so?

CHINADOLL. Don't you have one too?

RANDOLPH. I have too many.

CHINADOLL. Tell me one.

RANDOLPH. You don't know me. It won't mean anything.

CHINADOLL. I have seen many Americans come and go.

RANDOLPH. So I'm just one of them.

CHINADOLL. Just another tea trader.

RANDOLPH. If you know me so well, then tell me my secret.

(**RANDOLPH** *moves close.*)

CHINADOLL. A fly never visits an egg that is not cracked.

RANDOLPH. I heard you the first time.

CHINADOLL. You know what it means?

RANDOLPH. I'm not a cracked egg.

CHINADOLL. Did I say that?

RANDOLPH. If you knew my secret, I'd have to kill you.

(*A moment of uneasy tension, broken by* **RANDOLPH***'s laughter.*)

RANDOLPH. Can't you take a joke?

CHINADOLL. Not here. Not now. You don't know what's happening.

RANDOLPH. What is happening?

CHINADOLL. Many things. You have to learn fast. Otherwise…

(*Beat.*)

RANDOLPH. So, who are you, really?

CHINADOLL. I'll tell you my secret if you tell me yours.

RANDOLPH. How would I know you're telling the truth?

CHINADOLL. You just have to trust me.

RANDOLPH. And should I?

CHINADOLL. (*Turning to the audience*) It could have been so easy. The beautiful girl and the American who calls himself a fool. But he isn't a fool. And she's used to playing the same game too many times. Perhaps she cannot change. Perhaps it's all too late. So she leans in close, close enough for him to kiss her.

(**CHINADOLL** *does so. As he goes for it, she gently pulls away, but only slightly.*)

CHINADOLL. There is a time and place for everything.

RANDOLPH. I'm married. But I'm leaving her. Now your turn.

CHINADOLL. I don't love you.

(But she is lying, and he knows that.)

RANDOLPH. Good. I don't love you too.

(They kiss, as lights fade.)

End of Scene

Scene Four: Ambassador's Residence

(**AMBASSADOR**, *in a smoking jacket, sits next to an oil lamp, reading.*

There is a knock on the door.

He rises, heads towards the door and opens it.

SIMONE *enters. She appears tentative, unsure.*)

AMBASSADOR. What took you so long?

SIMONE. I saw something on the way here.

AMBASSADOR. Spare the excuse.

SIMONE. I'm not lying.

AMBASSADOR. Come here.

(*Only then does* **AMBASSADOR** *see that* **SIMONE** *is shaking.*)

SIMONE. It was terrible.

AMBASSADOR. What?

(*No response.*)

AMBASSADOR. Out with it.

SIMONE. I was taking a short cut, through this dark alley. I shouldn't have, but I did. Then suddenly a car drives past really quickly. I don't think they saw me. Otherwise they wouldn't have done it. It all happened so fast.

AMBASSADOR. What happened so fast?

SIMONE. I saw the men push something out of the backseat. I thought it was a sack. Like a sack of rice. But it was too big.

AMBASSADOR. A body?

SIMONE. It was a dead body.

AMBASSADOR. You sure it was dead?

SIMONE. There was blood all over. It was horrible. Horrible.

AMBASSADOR. (*Taking her in his arms*) Poor baby.

SIMONE. I don't know what to do. You have to help me. What should I do?

AMBASSADOR. Absolutely nothing. It's none of your business.

SIMONE. But...

AMBASSADOR. No buts. It's over. You're in my house. You're safe now.

SIMONE. I'm not.

AMBASSADOR. It's a bad shock. You'll get over it.

SIMONE. I think I know who he is.

AMBASSADOR. You said the body was in a sack.

SIMONE. The head. It popped out.

AMBASSADOR. You went up to have a look?

SIMONE. Well. I...

AMBASSADOR. You're a fool.

SIMONE. He has this distinctive mole on his cheek.

AMBASSADOR. With long white hair sprouting out of it?

SIMONE. Yes.

AMBASSADOR. You're quite sure? You said it was a dark alley.

SIMONE. I swear.

AMBASSADOR. This is bad.

SIMONE. It's Mr. Huang isn't it?

AMBASSADOR. May be.

SIMONE. What should we do?

AMBASSADOR. This is more serious than I thought.

SIMONE. You know about Mr. Huang?

(No response.)

SIMONE. Isn't he...

(She stops, not knowing what to say.)

AMBASSADOR. So, it has begun.

SIMONE. What has begun?

AMBASSADOR. The end of the Nationalists and their sympathizers.

SIMONE. *(Fearful)* What should I do? Tell me.

AMBASSADOR. What I know is not for your ears.

SIMONE. I'm in danger.

AMBASSADOR. Listen. Our relationship is strictly *business*. That's the arrangement.

SIMONE. *(Hurt)* Of course.

AMBASSADOR. But there's something you can do for me.

SIMONE. As long as I get my papers.

AMBASSADOR. You sound like a broken record. Do this for me and we see.

SIMONE. Do what?

AMBASSADOR. Find out the people in the car.

SIMONE. That's suicide. I may be a fool but I'm not stupid.

AMBASSADOR. Sometimes it's easier for a woman.

SIMONE. I'm not doing anything.

AMBASSADOR. Then kiss goodbye to your ticket out of Peking.

SIMONE. I'll do anything, anything but that.

AMBASSADOR. Then I'm sorry to say…

SIMONE. I'll be risking my life. And then what?

AMBASSADOR. How much are the papers worth to you?

(No response.)

AMBASSADOR. I would say quite a lot. *N'est-ce pas?*

(Beat. **SIMONE** *sees no way out of this.)*

SIMONE. All right.

AMBASSADOR. Good girl.

SIMONE. But I didn't see the people clearly.

AMBASSADOR. What was the automobile?

SIMONE. I don't know.

AMBASSADOR. Color?

SIMONE. Black. It was black.

AMBASSADOR. Distinctive markings?

SIMONE. No. I don't know.

AMBASSADOR. What about the men? How many?

SIMONE. I'm not sure. Three, maybe four.

AMBASSADOR. Locals, of course.

SIMONE. Yes. There was one, with a hat.

AMBASSADOR. A hat?

SIMONE. A western type of hat. Something like what you would wear.

AMBASSADOR. A Chinese who wears a western hat?

SIMONE. It's not so uncommon.

AMBASSADOR. You have someone in mind?

SIMONE. I said I couldn't see.

AMBASSADOR. But you saw the hat.

SIMONE. Everything was in shadows.

AMBASSADOR. But you suspect.

SIMONE. I don't suspect anything. How could I? I know nothing. I'm just a singer.

AMBASSADOR. Are you indeed? Then what are you doing here?

SIMONE. Because, well, because you need me.

(**AMBASSADOR** *laughs. The laughter turns lusty.*)

AMBASSADOR. So what are you waiting for?

SIMONE. I just saw a murder.

AMBASSADOR. You saw a dead body. The man could have died naturally.

SIMONE. That's not possible.

AMBASSADOR. Take off your clothes.

(*There is no response.*)

AMBASSADOR. Take them off.

SIMONE. The light is too bright.

(**AMBASSADOR** *turns down the oil lamp.*)

AMBASSADOR. Better?

(**SIMONE** *starts to disrobe. But before she goes very far, she breaks into sobs.*)

AMBASSADOR. Now what?

SIMONE. I can't.

AMBASSADOR. Of course you can.

SIMONE. I keep seeing his face.

AMBASSADOR. *(Flippant)* Not to mention the mole.

SIMONE. He was at the night club.

AMBASSADOR. What? When?

SIMONE. Tonight.

AMBASSADOR. When I was there?

SIMONE. No. Earlier.

AMBASSADOR. What was he doing?

SIMONE. Looking for someone. A foreign devil.

AMBASSADOR. You know who?

SIMONE. Younger than you. And more good looking.

AMBASSADOR. That's why you noticed.

SIMONE. Don't you want to know how I know?

AMBASSADOR. Not particularly.

SIMONE. They just missed each other. I have a good eye for such things.

AMBASSADOR. Who is this foreigner?

SIMONE. American.

AMBASSADOR. *Mon dieu.* Americans are imbeciles.

SIMONE. I thought they are your friends.

AMBASSADOR. They're certainly not my friends. They have no finesse in anything they do. No savoir faire.

SIMONE. I like Americans.

AMBASSADOR. Of course you do. You're as crass as any of them.

(**AMBASSADOR** *moves in, cups his hands under her breasts, and kisses her on the neck.*

SIMONE *melts under Ambassador's touch.*)

SIMONE. But I prefer Europeans.

AMBASSADOR. That's more like it.

SIMONE. Even if they are bastards.

AMBASSADOR. But you like bastards.

SIMONE. As long as they're nice to me.

(Just as the action gets started, there is a knock on the door.)

SIMONE. What was that?

(Beat. A louder knock.)

SIMONE. The door.

AMBASSADOR. *Merde.*

SIMONE. I'm afraid.

AMBASSADOR. What's there to be afraid of? Go in the other room. Put on your clothes.

SIMONE. I'd rather stay here.

AMBASSADOR. Do as I say. Now.

*(**SIMONE** gathers her things and exits.)*

AMBASSADOR. And don't come out until I say so.

*(**AMBASSADOR** goes to the door, opens it slowly.*

There is no one there.)

AMBASSADOR. Hullo? Anyone there?

*(As **AMBASSADOR** goes out, the door swings close. Lights fade.)*

End of Scene

Scene Five: Restaurant

(The same restaurant. The same after-hour ennui. And the same **CHINADOLL**, *smoking.*

She addresses the audience.)

CHINADOLL. When you see a beautiful girl alone in a restaurant, uneaten food in front of her, there can be many reasons. Perhaps she isn't hungry. Perhaps the food is bad. But ultimately, there can only be one *cause*. And that is fear. Fear that whatever she's doing will not lead to happiness. At least, not to the kind of happiness she's wished for ever since she was a girl. That which she has never known.

(Beat.)

Yesterday began like any other day. But it would end like no other. Her mission was simple. Go find the man. He would be at the Soiree at the Imperial Palace Gardens. Go talk to him. See what he's up to. The people he knows. The people he talks to. The beautiful girl knows what his goal is. It's all very simple. Contact will be made. Money will change hands. And something will happen. It's her job to prevent that.

(Beat.)

So the beautiful girl hid behind a peony bush. Not announcing her presence. Not yet. Just observing. Then, a Chinese man. A peculiar Chinese man, went up to the American. They spoke, no more than thirty seconds, and the man turned and left. It was then the beautiful girl saw his face. He had a mole. On his right cheek. A single long strand of hair sprouted from it. A face not easily forgotten. The beautiful girl quickly joined the American. But you know that already.

(Beat. She smiles.)

She knew this was going to be easy. Men are men, and this was no exception. She'd get everything she needed out of him. Even when his lips are sealed. Even when he could be put in jeopardy. You don't believe me?

(**RANDOLPH** *enters, as he was on the night of the Imperial Palace Gardens.*

CHINADOLL *leaves her cigarette to smolder, as we pick it up from the end of Scene Three.*)

CHINADOLL. There is a time and place for everything.

RANDOLPH. I'm married. But I'm leaving her. Now your turn.

CHINADOLL. I don't love you.

RANDOLPH. Good. I don't love you too.

CHINADOLL. It appears we're even.

RANDOLPH. And I thought I was ahead. So, what does one do at night in a place like this?

CHINADOLL. *(To audience)* She was waiting for the question. Almost expecting it at the moment he asked. The beautiful girl answered, nonchalant: *It depends on one's fancy. Beijing's not a city for night owls, unlike Shanghai.*

RANDOLPH. So what is your fancy?

CHINADOLL. The famous poet *Li Po* would say that the only thing a man needs on a night like this is the full moon.

RANDOLPH. But there's no full moon out. At least not that I can see. And that's too romantic a notion.

CHINADOLL. Do you think so? I think it's rather lonely.

RANDOLPH. Which is my point. Why be lonely in a city like this, when beauty is all around?

CHINADOLL. *So, will it be your place or mine?* *(To audience)* That was what the beautiful girl wanted to say. But she didn't. The words would not come out. Instead, she said: *Talking about beauty. The man with the mole, he looks really familiar. Isn't his name...*

RANDOLPH. Huang. His name is Huang.

CHINADOLL. *(To audience)* You see. He couldn't lie to her. It was that easy. Then, the beautiful girl turned back to the American, closer, feeling his warmth against hers, and said: *Beauty is indeed all around. Which is why I should leave you to enjoy it.* He was puzzled. I could see a question forming in his eyes.

RANDOLPH. But…

CHINADOLL. It is late. I had a good time.

RANDOLPH. So this is good night?

CHINADOLL. *(To audience)* It would have been too easy. And it wouldn't have changed anything. Or perhaps, it would have changed everything. But this was all part of the plan. So, it *was* good night. *Good night.*

(**RANDOLPH**, *crestfallen, exits.* **CHINADOLL** *sits back down, picks up her cigarette.*)

CHINADOLL. The feeling of sadness is nothing new to her, this beautiful girl. There are things more important than personal happiness. And alas, the beautiful girl knows what she must do. She must track down the man with the mole, and get rid of the mole.

(**CHINADOLL** *stubs her cigarette, as lights fade.*)

End of Scene

Scene Six: Ambassador's Residence

(A continuation of Scene Four.
Lights up. There is no one on stage.)

SIMONE *(O.S.)* Ambassador? Ambassador?

(SIMONE *enters, dressed in a silk robe.*
When she sees there is no one around, she starts to panic.
A sound offstage.)

SIMONE. Ambassador?

(The door opens. **RANDOLPH** *steps in, cautious.)*

SIMONE. Where's the Ambassador?

RANDOLPH. This is his house?

SIMONE. What have you done with him?

RANDOLPH. What do you mean?

SIMONE. Stay away from me.

RANDOLPH. My name is Randolph. I'm looking for the Ambassador.

SIMONE. Don't come near.

RANDOLPH. What's the matter?

SIMONE. Stay where you are.

*(***RANDOLPH** *stops.)*

RANDOLPH. All right. Tell me, what happened?

SIMONE. There was a knock on the door. He told me to stay in here. He went out. He didn't come back.

RANDOLPH. When was this?

SIMONE. Just now. Who are you?

RANDOLPH. As I said, my name is Randolph.

(Out of her confused state, **SIMONE** *finally realizes who* **RANDOLPH** *is.)*

SIMONE. You're the American. What do you want?

RANDOLPH. I just want to…who are you?

SIMONE. I'm a friend of the Ambassador.

RANDOLPH. A friend.

SIMONE. Yes.

RANDOLPH. Who was at the door?

SIMONE. I don't know.

RANDOLPH. Was the Ambassador expecting anyone?

SIMONE. No.

RANDOLPH. You're saying he's been abducted.

SIMONE. I don't know. I don't know what to think. You have to help me.

RANDOLPH. You look familiar.

SIMONE. I sing at the Peach Blossom Nightclub.

RANDOLPH. Of course. You sing beautifully.

SIMONE. Thank you. But it is just an act. It's *Zhou Xuan* singing, not me.

RANDOLPH. You fooled me.

SIMONE. I fool a lot of people. What should we do?

RANDOLPH. You said he went out the door and didn't come back.

SIMONE. Yes.

RANDOLPH. Stay here. Let me go out and look around.

SIMONE. Don't leave me alone here.

RANDOLPH. It'll be just a moment.

SIMONE. Come back quick.

(**RANDOLPH** *exits.* **SIMONE** *sits down and begins to cry.*

After a beat, **RANDOLPH** *re-enters.* **SIMONE** *turns to look.*)

RANDOLPH. He's gone.

(**RANDOLPH** *sees the state* **SIMONE** *is in.*)

RANDOLPH. Crying is not going to help.

(**RANDOLPH** *takes out a handkerchief and gives it to her.*)

RANDOLPH. Here.

SIMONE. Thank you.

RANDOLPH. This is what we're going to do. You're going to stay here and wait. When he comes back, please let me know. I'm staying at the Friendship Hotel. In the meantime I'm going to inform the authorities.

SIMONE. What if he doesn't come back?

RANDOLPH. You need to be calm. Can you do that?

(**SIMONE** *nods.*)

RANDOLPH. What's your name again?

SIMONE. Simone.

RANDOLPH. Simone. Good to meet you.

SIMONE. Good to meet you, too.

(**RANDOLPH** *turns to leave.* **SIMONE** *looks on, starts to sniffle again. But this time it is an act.*)

SIMONE. I'm so afraid. Why don't you stay awhile? I'd like you to.

(**RANDOLPH** *assesses the situation.*)

RANDOLPH. Thank you. But…

(Beat.)

SIMONE. *(Underplayed)* I can help you. No one needs to know.

RANDOLPH. Help me?

SIMONE. What if the Ambassador's dead? You could be next. I know Beijing inside out. There are many parts of the city white men don't go to. I can take you there. You'll be safe.

RANDOLPH. I am safe.

SIMONE. Are you so sure?

RANDOLPH. Let me be the judge of that.

SIMONE. There's one thing I should tell you.

RANDOLPH. Go on.

SIMONE. A little bird told me, the person you're looking for, is not in Beijing.

RANDOLPH. Who says I was looking for anyone?

SIMONE. No one knows where she is. Not even the bad guys.

(RANDOLPH takes a moment to think.)

RANDOLPH. What do you know?

SIMONE. Nothing. I know nothing.

RANDOLPH. This is about money isn't it?

SIMONE. I'm looking to get out of this country. Get me transit papers, and maybe I will help you.

RANDOLPH. You're trying too hard.

SIMONE. What options do you have?

RANDOLPH. I'll take my chances.

SIMONE. You know where to find me.

RANDOLPH. I don't intend to. Let me know when the Ambassador reappears.

SIMONE. Okay. I'll see you at Peach Blossom then.

RANDOLPH. I doubt it.

SIMONE. Trust me. We'll see each other again.

(RANDOLPH exits.)

SIMONE. Mr. Randolph Edward Dean. Tea trader.

(SIMONE lets out a little laugh, as lights fade.)

End of Scene

Scene Seven: Anonymous Building Corridor

(On two separate chairs sit **CHINADOLL** *and* **CHINESE MAN** *in a western hat.* **CHINESE MAN** *is smoking a cigarette. We hardly see his face.)*

CHINADOLL. At least we are making progress.

*(***CHINESE MAN** *takes another drag.)*

CHINADOLL. I'm moving as fast as I can. I need more time. Please.

(No response.)

CHINADOLL. The American is not a threat. At least not yet.

*(***CHINESE MAN** *clears his throat.)*

CHINADOLL. If you think… *(Long beat)* All right. I'll take care of him.

*(***CHINESE MAN** *smirks.)*

CHINADOLL. Maybe you're right. You do it. I know you love doing it.

*(***CHINESE MAN** *stands up.)*

CHINADOLL. So it's settled then?

*(***CHINESE MAN** *laughs.)*

CHINADOLL. *(To audience)* The beautiful girl hates his laugh. Always the same laugh. Conveying his contempt for the world. For the position he finds himself. The beautiful girl knows him only too well. Which is a good thing. For by suggesting he does the deed, she gets exactly what she wants.

*(***CHINESE MAN** *exits.)*

CHINADOLL. At least, her conscience is clear. That is what the beautiful girl tells herself. After all, she needs to believe in something. Anything. And now, she needs to find him. Set the plan in motion. The beautiful girl knows there are still too many steps ahead.

(Lights fade.)

End of Scene

Scene Eight: Interrogation Room

(Under harsh lights, **AMBASSADOR** *is being grilled by unseen interrogators. He is bound but defiant.)*

AMBASSADOR. You cannot do this to me! Haven't you heard of the Hague Convention?

(Beat. No response.)

Whatever you want, you will get nothing. This is not the way to treat an Ambassador. It's a grave infringement of diplomacy. My government will hear of this, and you will regret your actions. I demand that I'm released at once.

(There is no response. **AMBASSADOR** *struggles against his captivity.)*

Do you hear me? Release me at once. I told you I don't know anything about any film. Yes, I have a camera. Yes, I make little moving pictures. But that's my hobby. It has nothing to do with your absurd activity. And no, you may not watch my film. I have said more than enough. If I am not released this instant...

(Beat.)

Let me give you a simple lesson. When a person is the official representative of his country, a position called the Ambassador, you must accord him the highest privileges. But it is clear you know nothing of the sort. And that is very regrettable. Because once the proper authorities find out, there will be hell to pay.

(Beat.)

You cannot leave me alone here. Listen! Are you there? Is anybody there?!

(Lights fade as **AMBASSADOR** *continues to struggle.)*

End of Scene

Scene Nine: Randolph's Hotel Room

(It is night. Slivers of flashing neon visible through the window. Distant sounds of a Peking Opera.)

RANDOLPH *in bed, smoking, as* **CHINADOLL** *puts on a silk kimono. She stands next to a slowly rotating table fan, flickering light on her sad, beautiful face.)*

CHINADOLL. *(Almost to herself)* I shouldn't be here.

RANDOLPH. Isn't it what you want?

CHINADOLL. It's what you want.

*(***CHINADOLL** *takes a drink of water from a cut glass pitcher.)*

RANDOLPH. Come back to bed.

*(***CHINADOLL** *doesn't move.)*

RANDOLPH. What's the matter?

CHINADOLL. I'm going away.

RANDOLPH. Where? When?

CHINADOLL. Soon.

RANDOLPH. Where?

CHINADOLL. Does it matter?

(Beat.)

CHINADOLL. I'm not coming back.

RANDOLPH. What do you mean?

CHINADOLL. Just as I said.

RANDOLPH. Because you don't want to? Or because…

CHINADOLL. Why do you ask so many questions?

(Beat.)

CHINADOLL. You have to forget about me.

RANDOLPH. Is that what you want?

CHINADOLL. Yes, that's what I want.

*(***RANDOLPH** *gets out of bed and stubs out his cigarette. He looks out the window.)*

RANDOLPH. I won't.

(**CHINADOLL** *laughs a little laugh.*)

CHINADOLL. You Americans. You're all alike.

RANDOLPH. We're not all alike.

CHINADOLL. You're all alike.

(**CHINADOLL** *made her point.*)

RANDOLPH. I don't know anything about you.

CHINADOLL. There's nothing to know.

RANDOLPH. I want to.

(*There is no response.*)

RANDOLPH. What are your hobbies?

(*No response.*)

RANDOLPH. Your dreams?

(*No response.*)

RANDOLPH. What are you afraid of?

CHINADOLL. What makes you think…

(*Beat.*)

RANDOLPH. I can take you away from all this.

CHINADOLL. What?

RANDOLPH. Come with me.

(*Long beat.*)

CHINADOLL. I should go now.

(**CHINADOLL** *turns to leave.*)

RANDOLPH. What do you know about the Belgian Ambassador?

(**CHINADOLL** *stops, but she does not respond.*)

RANDOLPH. Where is he?

CHINADOLL. Is he missing?

RANDOLPH. Everyone's been talking about it.

(*Beat.*)

RANDOLPH. What is it you're not telling me?

(**CHINADOLL** *turns to the audience.*)

CHINADOLL. What is it that the beautiful girl isn't telling the American? She tells him what she wants to tell him. She tells him what he wants to hear. But there is one thing. The one thing he doesn't suspect. Otherwise he wouldn't be here, staring out the window. No. Not if he knew who the beautiful girl was.

RANDOLPH. Are you in some kind of trouble?

CHINADOLL. *(To audience)* She wants to say: *No, but you are.* But she stops herself. It would have given too much away. So she says: *No.*

RANDOLPH. You're not lying to me?

CHINADOLL. Why should I? *(To audience)* She cannot bear to break the boy's heart. Not yet. That comes later. Much later, after the beautiful girl has fallen in love with the boy. After when it is all too late.

(**RANDOLPH** *starts to dress.*)

RANDOLPH. I'm not a tea trader. Perhaps you figured it out by now.

(*There is no response.* **RANDOLPH** *finishes dressing up.*)

RANDOLPH. How can I find you?

CHINADOLL. You can't.

RANDOLPH. Please.

CHINADOLL. Let's just say good-bye.

RANDOLPH. No good-byes.

CHINADOLL. All right. No good-byes.

RANDOLPH. I'll find you.

CHINADOLL. *(Almost to herself)* No.

RANDOLPH. I'll find you.

CHINADOLL. *(To audience)* The beautiful girl stands there, not knowing what to say, yet knowing exactly what to say. She sees the man with his innocent eyes, so full of certainty and conviction, and for the first time, she feels something. That certain something. But as quickly as it comes, it goes away. It will not happen again, she tells herself. But she's only lying to herself. That's her weakness – lying to herself. And soon, she'll start paying for it.

(Lights fade.)

End of Scene

Scene Ten: Interrogation Room

(The same room. The same harsh light. **AMBASSADOR**, *still bound, now slumped. Next to him, a film projector, reels spinning, flickering, as the film is projected towards the audience.*

AMBASSADOR *wakes. He looks at the moving images, sighs, defeated. He addresses the audience.)*

When I woke up, the film was already playing. It was just me and the film. And the memories. Now, they're not even mine any more.

(Chinese Erhu music plays, softly.)

When I first came to Peking, there was hope. It was 1935. I was young. I fell in love. Then the war came. I went back to Europe. I wanted to take her. But it wasn't possible. When the war ended, I came back, looking for her. I thought, now things will begin again. Lives will begin again. Time, which has stopped, will start again. The skies, which have been dark, will become light again. And I, who was incomplete, will become complete. But she was gone. I looked everywhere. I followed all the leads. Every one of them. Eventually I found out. She was dead. Killed by the communists. Killed by her own people, the same bastards who are now keeping me against my will. I promised her. I promised myself. I will never deal with the communists. Let them kill me. Let them.

(Music fades. Beat.)

But I'm a coward. She's dead isn't she? What does anything matter anymore? We only have the living to consider. And that's the strategy isn't it: keep on living?

*(***AMBASSADOR*** watches the film.)*

I gave her all of my heart. And now I have no more.

(Beat, as lights slowly fade.)

End of Scene

Scene Eleven: Quiet Street

(Late night. Lights up on **RANDOLPH**, *wearing a hat and coat, walking down a deadly quiet alley in Beijing. There are shadows everywhere.)*

RANDOLPH. The time, after midnight. The place, a *hutong* in an unfamiliar part of Peking. I must have been walking for an hour. Not getting lost. Not going anywhere. I was drunk. That I knew. And I was alone. But that was about to change. Soon, a man, a Chinese man as far as I could tell, would step out of the shadows. He would be wearing a hat, tipped so low his face would not show. He'd be wearing a long coat, so that I couldn't tell his body shape, his musculature. And he'd be carrying a gun. But that I would not know till later. For now, he's still in the shadows. And here I was in the *hutong*, staring at the moon. And thinking about Chinadoll. *(Beat)* Chinadoll. Not her real name of course. It wouldn't have mattered what her name was. What happened to her? There was a part of me that longed to be with her. And there was another part… *(Beat)* She's trouble. She's that kind of trouble that wouldn't only take away a man's heart, but his…his everything. And I have a job to do. But wait. Wasn't I on my way to the Soiree? That was where I was going. How did I end up here? Nothing was making sense. The fact was, I was wandering the streets of the Imperial City with the moon as my only companion.

(He suddenly reacts to something.)

What was that sound? A cat? The rustling of sheets as someone turned over in his sleep? Or perhaps, a footfall.

(A sound.)

There it was again.

(A sound.)

And again. I was no longer alone. The Chinese man with the hat and the long coat. I crossed over to the other side of the *hutong*. He followed suit. I crossed back to the other side. He did so, discreetly, but deliberately.

I had a tail. If there was one thing I learnt in my line of work, it was this: avoid all possible confrontation. Run, hide, set up decoys. Do whatever you could to turn your status as a quarry into...

(**CHINESE MAN**, *wearing a hat and trench coat, enters. Facing away, he takes out a cigarette and lights it.*)

RANDOLPH. There he was. Lighting a cigarette as he moved along the alleyway. As the lighter flared, for a moment, I could see his face. Or at least, I thought I could see it. What did the face tell me? I wasn't sure. There was no reading him. But that must be it. I *was* drunk. Wasn't I drinking before this? At the bar. Where was that place? What was I drinking? What was in the drink? I see. There was something in the drink.

(**CHINESE MAN**, *still in the shadows, moves closer.*)

The man took a puff of his cigarette. Exhaling, I could see the smoke catching glints of the moonlight, like it was snowing, in slow motion, upwards instead of down. Then, this feeling. Was it panic? I wasn't sure. I felt something. Something urgent. It wouldn't go away. It kept me rooted to the spot. The Chinaman approached, slowly. He took out his gun.

(**CHINESE MAN** *does so.*)

He aimed. He fired.

(*A BANG. Dogs begin to bark.*)

And I stood there, in shock, until I felt blood on my shirt.

(**RANDOLPH** *slowly collapses onto the ground.*)

RANDOLPH. I cannot die here. That was my thought. I cannot die before my mission is done. I cannot die till I see Chinadoll again.

(**RANDOLPH** *passes out.* **CHINESE MAN** *removes his hat and steps into the light, revealing* **CHINADOLL**, *as lights fade.*)

End of Scene

End of Act I

Scene Twelve: Hospital

(Lights up showing **RANDOLPH** *on a hospital bed, asleep.*

Next to him in a chair, **AMBASSADOR**, *almost blending into the hospital decor.*

Nothing happens for a while. Then **RANDOLPH** *coughs fitfully, awakes.*

He looks groggily around him. His eyes land on Ambassador.)

RANDOLPH. Do I know you?

AMBASSADOR. Perhaps you do. Perhaps you don't.

RANDOLPH. You look…familiar. Your accent.

AMBASSADOR. What about my accent?

RANDOLPH. It's French, right?

AMBASSADOR. Belgian.

RANDOLPH. I think I know who you are.

AMBASSADOR. I'm here to deliver a message. *(Beat)* The truth is, you're lucky to be alive.

RANDOLPH. That's the message?

AMBASSADOR. That could be the message, but no.

(Beat.)

RANDOLPH. Well?

(AMBASSADOR *takes out a cigarette, lights it and starts to smoke.)*

AMBASSADOR. Let me put it this way. I place myself in an awkward position to tell you what I will tell you.

RANDOLPH. Then don't.

AMBASSADOR. Yet I must.

RANDOLPH. This is too complicated. Thank you for coming. But I must rest.

*(***AMBASSADOR** *contemplates the situation.)*

AMBASSADOR. I know who tried to kill you.

RANDOLPH. I already know, thank you. We've started an official investigation.

AMBASSADOR. They won't find anything.

RANDOLPH. What makes you so sure?

AMBASSADOR. Because they have the wrong evidence.

(Randolph's interest is piqued.)

RANDOLPH. Tell me more.

AMBASSADOR. The person who shot you, was a woman.

RANDOLPH. It was a man. I saw him following me.

AMBASSADOR. You are so sure. You were drugged, weren't you?

RANDOLPH. I think I can tell a man from a woman.

AMBASSADOR. She's dangerous.

RANDOLPH. What's the point of this?

AMBASSADOR. You're not safe. You have to leave the country.

RANDOLPH. And if I don't?

AMBASSADOR. Then maybe *I* will have to kill you. I don't want to, of course. But, maybe I have no choice.

RANDOLPH. I don't understand.

AMBASSADOR. I don't blame you. You see, I made a deal with the devil.

RANDOLPH. And by the devil you mean…

AMBASSADOR. I think it's obvious enough.

RANDOLPH. I see. It's not my problem.

AMBASSADOR. Your life is not your problem?

(The thought sinks in.)

RANDOLPH. So by telling me this…

AMBASSADOR. You leave Peking. That's what they want.

RANDOLPH. Then I'm making better progress than I thought.

AMBASSADOR. You don't realize the danger you're in.

RANDOLPH. I was almost killed. I think I understand the situation.

AMBASSADOR. Things will only get worse.

RANDOLPH. How much are they paying you?

AMBASSADOR. It's not that simple.

RANDOLPH. You're not answering the question.

AMBASSADOR. And you're not listening.

RANDOLPH. I've had enough of this. Tell them they're wasting their time.

AMBASSADOR. It can be very simple. I accidently drop this cigarette here. Something catches fire. There will be no escape.

RANDOLPH. Then do it.

(*Beat.* **AMBASSADOR** *sighs, turns to leave.*

RANDOLPH *suddenly remembers something.*)

RANDOLPH. I have been to your house.

(**AMBASSADOR** *turns round.*)

AMBASSADOR. You've been to my house? Here, in Peking?

RANDOLPH. You weren't there. I met… Simone.

AMBASSADOR. And?

RANDOLPH. You were missing. We looked for you.

AMBASSADOR. And?

RANDOLPH. We didn't find you.

AMBASSADOR. Clearly not.

RANDOLPH. She *said* something.

AMBASSADOR. (*Suspicious*) About?

RANDOLPH. The person I'm looking for…

AMBASSADOR. (*Quickly interjecting*) Not here.

RANDOLPH. And now you want to kill me.

AMBASSADOR. Things change. What matters is that you leave. As soon as possible.

RANDOLPH. So, a *woman* tried to kill me. Why would you say such a thing?

AMBASSADOR. Because it's the truth. And because you know who she is.

RANDOLPH. Is that so?

AMBASSADOR. If you think clearly, you'll realize what happened. And you will listen to me.

RANDOLPH. Thank you for your pearls of wisdom.

(**AMBASSADOR** *turns to leave. After a beat, he turns back.*)

AMBASSADOR. You're a smart man.

RANDOLPH. That we can both agree on.

AMBASSADOR. The next time I see you, things will be different.

RANDOLPH. You don't scare me.

AMBASSADOR. Good bye, *mon ami.*

RANDOLPH. May you rot in hell.

AMBASSADOR. I'm already in hell.

(**AMBASSADOR** *stubs out his cigarette.*)

And so are you. You just don't know it yet.

(*Lights fade, as* **AMBASSADOR** *exits.*)

End of Scene

Scene Thirteen: Restaurant

(The same restaurant as Scene One. Late evening.)

SIMONE, *bored, nursing a cup of tea.*

CHINADOLL *enters.* **SIMONE** *does a double take. They don't acknowledge each other.*

CHINADOLL *sits.)*

CHINADOLL. Where's the waiter?

SIMONE. I don't know. *(Beat)* It's almost closing time.

CHINADOLL. I'm a regular here.

SIMONE. So am I.

*(**CHINADOLL** *eyes* **SIMONE** *suspiciously.)*

SIMONE. I've not seen you around.

CHINADOLL. Are you here from the time they open to the time they close?

SIMONE. No.

CHINADOLL. Clearly not.

SIMONE. Why are you lying?

*(**CHINADOLL**, *now on edge, looks sharply at* **SIMONE**.*)*

SIMONE. Why do you say you're a regular when you're not?

CHINADOLL. Who are you?

SIMONE. I'm the one looking for you.

CHINADOLL. What is your purpose?

SIMONE. This.

*(**SIMONE** *takes out a gun and points it at* **CHINADOLL**, *who merely smiles.)*

CHINADOLL. You're not the only person wanting me dead.

SIMONE. But I'm the one who'll make sure you are.

CHINADOLL. If only it were so easy.

SIMONE. Watch me.

*(**SIMONE** *takes aim, but before she can shoot,* **CHINA-DOLL** *takes out a pistol of her own.)*

(It is a standoff.)

CHINADOLL. I'm watching.

(A tense beat.

Just then, the **WAITER** *enters, carrying a tray. On seeing what is happening, he drops it on the floor and runs out.)*

SIMONE. Looks like there's no service for you.

CHINADOLL. *(Nonchalant)* Who put you up to this?

SIMONE. That's none of your business.

CHINADOLL. If I'm to be killed, I'd like to know who's behind it.

SIMONE. What makes you think there's more than just me?

CHINADOLL. I wasn't born yesterday.

SIMONE. If you're so smart, figure it out for yourself.

CHINADOLL. For one thing, I know who you are. I knew when I stepped into the restaurant.

SIMONE. Well, that's not too surprising. I am a famous singer after all.

CHINADOLL. Hardly famous. And that place of disrepute you perform in? A disgrace to the people of China.

SIMONE. Then why do people pay to see me?

CHINADOLL. They're not people. Just foreign devils. And you're not a singer. You're just a, how shall I put it, a capitalist. The worst sort.

SIMONE. I take that as a compliment.

CHINADOLL. It's people like you who drag China down.

SIMONE. And you? How many people have the Red Army killed?

CHINADOLL. It's a means to an end.

SIMONE. What end? Tell me? By the time Mao is through, there won't be any of us left.

CHINADOLL. You're buying into the white man's propaganda.

SIMONE. Karl Marx is a white man too.

CHINADOLL. You are so ignorant.

SIMONE. And you know so much.

(*Beat.*)

SIMONE. So we're just going to stand here and point at each other?

CHINADOLL. You have a better suggestion?

(**SIMONE**'s *hand gets tired. She changes hand.* **CHINADOLL** *smirks.*)

CHINADOLL. Ambidextrous?

SIMONE. As a matter of fact, I am.

CHINADOLL. You make me laugh. You hang around a lot with that Belgian clown of an ambassador don't you?

SIMONE. I don't know what you're talking about.

CHINADOLL. You give it away too easily.

SIMONE. So what if I did?

CHINADOLL. He put you up to this.

SIMONE. Why would he?

CHINADOLL. I know him. You know that?

(*No response.*

CHINADOLL *smiles, starts to move closer. As she does so,* **SIMONE** *moves away. The two women begin to circle each other.*)

CHINADOLL. He has always relied on foolish girls who want nothing more than promises of jade mountains and golden dragons. He's a gutless, desperate buffoon. No better than a Qing eunuch.

SIMONE. He's a good man.

CHINADOLL. You sadden me. This is what the motherland has become.

SIMONE. Actually there's a little difference between us. You follow Mao, and I follow the rest of the world. Somehow, I think the rest of the world is going to win.

CHINADOLL. And if it doesn't?

SIMONE. I'll be dead long before it's decided one way or the other.

CHINADOLL. Yet here you are, holding a gun, ready to do a dog's bidding.

(There's no response.)

CHINADOLL. It's not too late you know. To repent. To accept Mao into your life. Don't you want to change the world for the better? Don't you dream about justice and fairness and comradeship? China should be the strongest nation in the world, and yet, we are nowhere. But things are about to change. You don't want to be left behind.

SIMONE. My destiny is not here.

CHINADOLL. What makes you so sure? Maybe your destiny is to run into someone in a restaurant who will convince you there's something better out there.

SIMONE. How very likely.

CHINADOLL. Stranger things have happened. I was like you once. A petty, petulant little thing. But when I listened to Mao speak, my world changed. I was finally able to open my eyes and see. I was liberated from the chains of my bourgeois thinking.

SIMONE. "Chains of bourgeois thinking"? That doesn't sound like a real person talking.

CHINADOLL. Take my advice. Go listen to Mao. You don't know what you're missing.

SIMONE. I'm not interested.

CHINADOLL. He's coming to a village not too far from here. If persuaded, I might even be kind enough to arrange a little trip for you.

SIMONE. I'm not falling for that.

CHINADOLL. Put down your gun.

(No reaction.)

CHINADOLL. Put it down.

SIMONE. I'll put it down if you do the same.

CHINADOLL. We'll do it together. At the count of three.

One, two, three.

(Both guns are lowered.)

CHINADOLL. That's much better.

(With the relief, a flood of tears comes to **SIMONE**.*)*

SIMONE. I just wanted to get those transit papers. I don't know what I was doing. I think I'm going crazy.

CHINADOLL. You're not going crazy. Things are going to be all right.

SIMONE. What should I do now?

CHINADOLL. Time to open your mind to new things.

SIMONE. You think so?

CHINADOLL. Meet me by the West Gate. Friday. Six o'clock sharp.

*(***SIMONE** *composes herself.* **CHINADOLL** *turns to leave.)*

SIMONE. What should I wear?

CHINADOLL. Wear your proudest face. Wear your patriotic heart on your sleeve. Wear it like our warrior ancestors. This is a new beginning. Your life starts now.

(Lights fade.)

End of Scene

Scene Fourteen: Randolph's Hotel Room

(**RANDOLPH**, *in bandages, enters, carrying a bag containing his belongings.*

Late afternoon sun slants in through the window.

As he sets down his bag on the table, a puff of dust forms. He has been gone a long time. He turns on the table fan.

There is a knock on the door. **RANDOLPH** *stiffens. After a beat, there is another knock.*)

HOTEL CLERK *(O.S.)* Letter.

RANDOLPH. What?

HOTEL CLERK *(O.S.)* A letter for Mr. Randolph.

RANDOLPH. Slip it under the door.

(**HOTEL CLERK** *does so.* **RANDOLPH** *retrieves the letter.*

He goes to the bed, ripping open the envelope and starts to read.)

RANDOLPH. Dear Randolph. By the time you receive this letter, I will have gone. Your being away – it has been hard on me, too hard perhaps, and I am weak. You know that I need someone around to share my thoughts. Someone next to me in bed. Our bed. I'm only now beginning to understand what you do. Or at least, I pretend to. But I've made a decision, Randolph. I cannot live like this. I cannot wait for you. I suppose there are women out there who would do this in the name of our country. How noble that is. But alas, I'm not one of them. I'm very proud of you, Randolph, and I will always love you, but I cannot be your wife. Love, Lanie.

(**RANDOLPH** *sighs, folds up the letter and sets it aside. He lies on the bed, deep in thought.*

Soft, indistinct music begins to play. The music slowly becomes louder. It is "In a Sentimental Mood."

*As **RANDOLPH** gets lost in the music, **CHINADOLL** appears, almost as if by magic.*

*Soon **RANDOLPH** notices her, and bolts straight up.)*

RANDOLPH. What are you doing here?

CHINADOLL. I'm not really here. Just a figment of your imagination.

RANDOLPH. The music.

CHINADOLL. The very tune we danced to at the Imperial Palace Gardens.

RANDOLPH. I must be going out of my mind.

CHINADOLL. You're still under medication. It's not an uncommon side effect.

RANDOLPH. You're beautiful as always.

CHINADOLL. You don't see what's inside.

RANDOLPH. Where have you been?

CHINADOLL. Everywhere. Nowhere.

(Beat.)

RANDOLPH. I know.

CHINADOLL. Know what?

RANDOLPH. It was you, wasn't it?

CHINADOLL. That's a very vague question.

RANDOLPH. It's not vague at all.

(Beat.)

CHINADOLL. You're accusing me of… but I'm just an apparition. An apparition conjured up by you. You can put any words in my mouth.

RANDOLPH. Why? Why did you try to kill me?

CHINADOLL. Did I? I didn't kill you. You're not dead.

RANDOLPH. Right, but…

CHINADOLL. What motives do I have?

RANDOLPH. You were seen at a Mao rally, with Simone.

CHINADOLL. Just taking in the scenery.

RANDOLPH. That's a lousy excuse and you know it.

CHINADOLL. Then give me a better one.

RANDOLPH. I was wrong about you.

CHINADOLL. You're still so new to China. It's sad, really. I'd expected more of you.

RANDOLPH. You're just a dirty communist bitch.

(**CHINADOLL** *laughs.*)

CHINADOLL. So this is what it's about.

RANDOLPH. You're not going to deny it?

CHINADOLL. Feel free to put words in my mouth. Anything you want.

*(No response from **RANDOLPH**.)*

CHINADOLL. All right. I'll say 'yes.' Then what? You kill me? You can if you want to. But what if I said 'no'? Would you continue to love me? Is that what you want? You really are confused aren't you?

RANDOLPH. Don't play games with me. Just tell me the truth.

CHINADOLL. There's no truth. Not here in Beijing. You know better than that. There are only various shades of grey.

RANDOLPH. But I didn't die. It would have been so easy.

CHINADOLL. Let's just say I missed.

RANDOLPH. You didn't miss. You intended it all along.

CHINADOLL. Seems very complicated.

RANDOLPH. What is it that I'm missing?

CHINADOLL. You're a smart man.

RANDOLPH. I'm not looking for compliments.

CHINADOLL. And I'm not giving one. Just speaking your thoughts. Shall I go now?

RANDOLPH. Come here.

(**CHINADOLL** *does so.*)

CHINADOLL. *(Smiling)* This fantasy is taking on a decidedly interesting turn.

(**RANDOLPH** *begins to say something, but* **CHINADOLL** *hushes him by putting her finger on his lips.*)

CHINADOLL. You have such soft lips.

(**RANDOLPH** *nibbles at her fingers.*)

CHINADOLL. You like that?

RANDOLPH. What do you know about "The Twins"?

(**CHINADOLL** *doesn't even miss a beat.*)

CHINADOLL. You have such beautiful eyes.

RANDOLPH. Talk to me.

CHINADOLL. The time for talking is passed.

(**CHINADOLL** *starts to unbutton* **RANDOLPH**'s *shirt.*)

CHINADOLL. Now, isn't that better?

(Lights slowly fade.

Beat. As lights go up again, **CHINADOLL** *is gone.*

In her place, an old FILM CAN.

At this point, the next scene begins and overlaps.

RANDOLPH *opens the can and discovers a tiny spool of film. Unfurling the strip, he holds it up against the lights, viewing with great interest.)*

End of Scene

Scene Fifteen: Alleyway

(Adjacent to Randolph's hotel.

Night is falling.

CHINESE BUSINESSMAN *runs in with a briefcase. He is panting, panic-stricken.*

Running into a blind alley, **CHINESE BUSINESSMAN** *is trapped. He doesn't know what to do.*

Out of the shadows, a figure enters. It is **AMBASSADOR**.

We can just make out he is holding a gun.

As **AMBASSADOR** *moves near,* **CHINESE BUSINESSMAN**, *now in tears, crumples onto the ground.)*

AMBASSADOR. That's why they call you the "Businessman." Now I understand. You take my money. You get me the film. Then somebody offers you more money. You take away the film. THE FILM IS MINE. In case you do not realize, the communist pigs and I have an understanding. That's why they returned me the film. Now, the film disappears, again. And you say it is "them." But they insist they don't have it. So who's lying? It's obvious isn't it? Who's the highest bidder this time?

*(***AMBASSADOR** *advances even closer.)*

I'm a very patient man. But now I run out of patience. I count to three. One.

*(***CHINESE BUSINESSMAN** *shakes his head vigorously.)*

AMBASSADOR. Two.

*(***CHINESE BUSINESSMAN** *continues to shake his head.)*

You do not value your life that much do you? All I need is a name. *(Beat)* No? How do you say it in Mandarin? Three – *san?*

(Just as **AMBASSADOR** *readies to shoot,* **CHINESE BUSINESSMAN** *rushes at him, screaming.*

The two wrestle, trying to gain control of the weapon. Suddenly it goes off, firing harmlessly into the air.

CHINESE BUSINESSMAN *takes this opportunity to slink away into the night.*

Meanwhile, **RANDOLPH** *hears the shot, reacts.*

AMBASSADOR, *about to follow* **CHINESE BUSINESSMAN**, *notices the latter's briefcase sitting on the ground. He opens it, rifles through the content, but finds nothing of interest.*

RANDOLPH *exits his room to investigate.*

AMBASSADOR *exits in pursuit of* **CHINESE BUSINESSMAN**.

Moments later **RANDOLPH** *enters the alleyway. He surveys the scene, spots the open briefcase, goes up to examine it.*

From within the briefcase, he fishes out a LITTLE RED BOOK. He looks at it, trying to figure out what happened, as lights slowly fade.)

End of Scene

Scene Sixteen: Nightclub Dressing Room

(**SIMONE**, *putting on make-up, is preparing to take the stage. Jazz music filters from without.*

Then, a noise. She looks around, sees nothing. She continues to apply her make-up.

CHINESE MAN *with hat and trench coat enters surreptitiously. It takes a moment for* **SIMONE** *to register. She freezes, then decides to put on a brave front.*)

SIMONE. If you want my autograph, you'll have to wait till after my performance.

(No response. **CHINESE MAN** *moves closer.)*

Stay where you are. If you don't leave at once, I will scream.

(Still no response. **CHINESE MAN** *tips his hat even lower.)*

You think I'm stupid right? I know who you are. I know why you're here. And you know what, I'm not frightened.

(**CHINESE MAN** *moves to take something out of his coat.* **SIMONE**'s *facade crumbles.*)

SIMONE. Please, don't. PLEASE! I will cooperate. I will do whatever you want. I don't want to die.

(**CHINESE MAN** *laughs, withdraws his hand. He moves close to* **SIMONE**, *feels her up. She is shaking.*)

I know a lot of people. I can get you information that no one else can get. I'm much more useful to you alive than dead.

(No response.)

For example, I know that the wife of the Italian Commissioner is addicted to opium and sleeping with her chauffeur. The Argentine diplomats host an orgy every Sunday night at their embassy. And the Burmese ambassador is very interested in young boys.

(**CHINESE MAN** *holds up* **SIMONE**'s *chin, contemplating his next move.*)

SIMONE. Also, I know an ambassador out there who may be willing to support Mao, in return for... well, it can be discussed. My set is about to begin. I need to get ready.

(*She tries to stand up, but* **CHINESE MAN** *won't let her.*)

Please.

(*Again she tries to get up, and again he thwarts her.*)

They'll know something is wrong.

(**CHINESE MAN** *take outs a garrote.* **SIMONE** *screams.*

At that moment, **RANDOLPH** *enters. He is pointing a gun at* **CHINESE MAN**.)

RANDOLPH. Drop it.

(*No response.*)

I said, drop it. Put your arms in the air. NOW.

(**CHINESE MAN** *does so.* **RANDOLPH** *moves to pat down the man.*)

SIMONE. It's you.

RANDOLPH. I'm not here to help you.

(**CHINESE MAN** *seizes the moment to lunge at* **RANDOLPH**, *who quickly sidesteps. With one jab,* **CHINESE MAN** *is knocked out cold.*)

SIMONE. Impressive.

RANDOLPH. I need rope to tie him up.

SIMONE. Why not just kill him?

RANDOLPH. I can't do that.

SIMONE. That was a joke.

RANDOLPH. It's not funny.

(**SIMONE** *looks around for rope. She doesn't find any.*)

RANDOLPH. Give me a hand will you?

(**RANDOLPH** *and* **SIMONE** *drag* **CHINESE MAN** *offstage and re-enter.*)

SIMONE. I really need to go.
RANDOLPH. I've got to talk to you.
SIMONE. Afterwards.
RANDOLPH. Where's the Ambassador?
SIMONE. I don't know.
RANDOLPH. I know you do.
SIMONE. I cannot help you.
RANDOLPH. Don't make me force you.
SIMONE. Is that a threat?
RANDOLPH. Could be.
SIMONE. You're no better than the communist dog. I'm disappointed.
RANDOLPH. You're wasting my time. Just tell me where he is.
SIMONE. What's in it for me?

(**RANDOLPH** *takes out a document from his jacket but does not give it to* **SIMONE**.)

RANDOLPH. This.
SIMONE. Transit papers!
RANDOLPH. You have five seconds.
SIMONE. All right. You win. You can find him…

(**AMBASSADOR** *appears.* **RANDOLPH** *keeps the transit papers.*)

AMBASSADOR. *(Interjecting)* You can find him here. So you didn't leave Peking. Very unwise.
RANDOLPH. I've a mystery to solve.
AMBASSADOR. So you're suddenly Sherlock Holmes.
RANDOLPH. I need to find her. I think you know where she is.

(**AMBASSADOR** *laughs.*)

AMBASSADOR. You surprise me. A romantic.
RANDOLPH. I'm not talking about Chinadoll.

(*There is no response from* **AMBASSADOR**.)

RANDOLPH. I know about the film.

> (**AMBASSADOR** *disguises his surprise.* **SIMONE** *senses something is not right.*)

SIMONE. What film?

RANDOLPH. *(Playing her)* You don't know?

SIMONE. *(To* **AMBASSADOR***)* What film?

AMBASSADOR. There's no film.

SIMONE. I don't believe you.

RANDOLPH. It's from before the war. When he was first here. A film about his Chinese mistress.

SIMONE. *(To* **AMBASSADOR***)* You didn't tell me any of this.

RANDOLPH. Of course not.

AMBASSADOR. *(To* **SIMONE***)* It's none of your business.

SIMONE. What else don't I know?

RANDOLPH. Maybe he can tell you what happened to her.

AMBASSADOR. She disappeared.

RANDOLPH. She died. And how did she die?

AMBASSADOR. That is enough.

SIMONE. I want to know.

AMBASSADOR. *(To* **RANDOLPH***)* Don't you get it? This is all part of the communist plan, to create doubt, mistrust, division between allies like us.

RANDOLPH. This from someone who's trying to kill me.

SIMONE. *(To* **AMBASSADOR***)* You're trying to kill him?

AMBASSADOR. Shut up.

SIMONE. *(To* **RANDOLPH***)* I don't know what to think.

AMBASSADOR. It doesn't matter what you think. All you want are your papers.

SIMONE. No, this is about us.

AMBASSADOR. "Us"? There is an "us"?

> (**SIMONE** *breaks into sobs.*)

AMBASSADOR. *(To* **RANDOLPH**; *aside)* So *you* took the film.

RANDOLPH. I don't have the film.

(**AMBASSADOR** *is stumped.*)

RANDOLPH. You could have taken her away with you, to Belgium, when the war came. But you didn't. You left her here to die.

AMBASSADOR. That's absurd. Completely absurd.

RANDOLPH. Then why do you feel so guilty?

AMBASSADOR. I don't. I loved her.

SIMONE. That's why you don't talk about before the war. You never talk about before the war.

AMBASSADOR. The memories are too painful. But it wasn't because of me that she was killed.

RANDOLPH. So your deal with the devil…

AMBASSADOR. She made me promise, not to tell anyone she has a sister. A *twin* sister. Because if they found out, that was the end.

SIMONE. The twins! But I don't understand. Why would anyone want to kill both sisters?

AMBASSADOR. Not anyone. "Them." Because the sisters were communists, *and* agents for the Americans at the same time.

(*To* **RANDOLPH**)

Right?

(*Beat.*)

AMBASSADOR. That's your purpose in Peking isn't it? To smuggle her out of this country. Something you should have done long ago.

RANDOLPH. Except the war came.

AMBASSADOR. Then you're just using the same excuse as I.

(**AMBASSADOR** *takes out a gun, and points it at* **RANDOLPH**.)

RANDOLPH. So it's her life for my life.

AMBASSADOR. It's a fair exchange.

(*A BANG, and* **AMBASSADOR** *crumbles to the floor.*)

(**CHINADOLL** *enters, a smoking gun in her hand.*

SIMONE, *in tears, tends to* **AMBASSADOR**.*)*

RANDOLPH. *(To* **CHINADOLL***)* I guess I owe you one.

CHINADOLL. No you don't.

SIMONE. He's dead.

CHINADOLL. A most fitting end.

SIMONE. He mentioned the twins before. But I didn't think he was talking about before the war. I wasn't in Beijing then.

CHINADOLL. That's why he chose you. *(To* **RANDOLPH***)* Let's go. There's not much time.

RANDOLPH. Where are we going?

CHINADOLL. Follow me. Everything will be clear.

RANDOLPH. *(To* **SIMONE***)* Call the police. Can you do that?

SIMONE. *(Still dazed)* What am I going to say?

CHINADOLL. You're a smart girl. You'll think of something.

(**RANDOLPH** *hands over the transit papers to* **SIMONE**.*)*

RANDOLPH. Here, the papers. Take care of yourself.

SIMONE. Okay.

RANDOLPH. *(To* **CHINADOLL***)* Somehow I knew you'd come through for me.

CHINADOLL. Don't forget I'm still a communist.

RANDOLPH. I take a woman who draws a gun very seriously.

(**CHINADOLL** *smiles.*)

CHINADOLL. You like watching films?

RANDOLPH. Any one in particular?

CHINADOLL. You'll like this one. Come.

(**CHINADOLL** *and* **RANDOLPH** *exit.*

SIMONE *crouches over* **AMBASSADOR***'s dead body, stroking his face, looking forlorn. Suddenly, seized by a thought, she takes her transit papers and proceeds to shred them into bits, tears rolling down her cheeks as she does so.*

As she lies down next to **AMBASSADOR**, *lights slowly fade.)*

End of Scene

Scene Seventeen: Residence In Village Near Beijing

(A place that has seen better days. A white sheet hangs, serving as make-shift projection screen. A slight breeze makes it ripple like silk.

PROJECTED:

A black-and-white silent film, home-made, showing Ambassador and his mistress.

They loll about in a beautiful Chinese garden, talking, smiling.

We zoom in as they move in close to kiss. Then the film freezes, just as their lips are about to touch.

Lights go up. We see that there is a **WOMAN** *watching the film. She faces away from the audience. We do not see her face.*

The woman's hair is wild. She is smoking opium.

CHINADOLL *enters with* **RANDOLPH**. *She lets him have a moment to take in the scene.)*

CHINADOLL. *(Referring to the film)* They were a beautiful couple.

RANDOLPH. Our Belgian Ambassador.

CHINADOLL. He wasn't Ambassador then.

RANDOLPH. I knew it was you who left the little souvenir in my room.

(**CHINADOLL** *smiles, but says nothing.)*

RANDOLPH. *(Watching the film)* That was what, ten years ago?

CHINADOLL. Just about. Then the war came.

RANDOLPH. Isn't it strange how, one day, we're fighting the far right, and the next, the far left?

CHINADOLL. Americans meddle too much.

RANDOLPH. There are principles to uphold.

CHINADOLL. And what are these principles?

RANDOLPH. *(Smiles)* Are you interrogating me?

CHINADOLL. Maybe I am.

RANDOLPH. So this is the woman in question.

CHINADOLL. One half of the twins. She's not well.

(**RANDOLPH** *surveys the place.*)

RANDOLPH. How did you know this is what I have to do?

CHINADOLL. Does it matter? I'm giving her to you on a platter.

RANDOLPH. Platter? You've been keeping her under house arrest. We tried, you know, getting her out, when it was clear…

CHINADOLL. You didn't try hard enough.

RANDOLPH. Things were different then. But now. *(Beat)* Let's get down to business. What would it take for me to get her away?

CHINADOLL. Nothing. She's free to go.

RANDOLPH. I don't understand.

CHINADOLL. I'm just looking after her.

RANDOLPH. Looking after? This house is well hidden. I wouldn't have found it myself. No one would.

CHINADOLL. That's exactly the point. No one knows she's here. Not even my comrades.

RANDOLPH. Let's say I'm a bit dense. What's the catch?

CHINADOLL. I thought you'd have figured it out by now. She's my mother's sister.

(The revelation slowly sinks in.)

RANDOLPH. *(Looking at the film)* Your mother's beautiful.

CHINADOLL. Yes she was.

(**CHINADOLL** *goes up to* **WOMAN**, *gently removes the opium pipe, and attempts to straighten her hair.*)

RANDOLPH. That's why you didn't kill me. You knew what I had to do all along.

(**CHINADOLL** *combs for a bit, not responding, then turns to the audience.*)

CHINADOLL. The beautiful girl wants to say something.

Something to refute that statement. That that is the only reason she didn't kill him. That there isn't something else. But she couldn't. It's not about her now. It's about her mother's sister. And the wishes of a beautiful dead woman. The time for feelings is long past. So, with a twinge of sadness, she turns to him and says: *Now you know. Please take good care of her. She's had a hard life.*

(**RANDOLPH** *nods.*)

RANDOLPH. I wish things could be different.

CHINADOLL. Your mission's done.

RANDOLPH. So is yours. What will you do now?

CHINADOLL. *(To audience)* Is the beautiful girl reading too much into that simple question? Is he asking her if she wanted to go with him? What if he did? What would she say? All she knows is, she has finally carried out her mother's dying wish. She's finally free. And now, she needs to go back to doing her job. Which is what she says: *I have a job to do.*

RANDOLPH. A job.

CHINADOLL. Actually it's more than a job. It's a cause.

RANDOLPH. A cause I don't understand.

CHINADOLL. That's our difference.

RANDOLPH. And yet, we're so similar, in so many ways.

(*Beat.* **RANDOLPH** *turns to address the audience.*)

RANDOLPH. She asked me about principles. I have a theory about that. It all boils down to doing the right thing. That's all there really is to know. You see, she wants to change the world. And I just want to do the right thing. I cannot allow history to repeat itself. Not on my watch. Not even if my life's on the line. That's why I'm here. And that's why we're always there, when there's trouble. Because we do the right thing. *(Looking at* **CHINADOLL***)* I think she appreciates that.

(*Suddenly, the film resumes, except now in SLOW*

MOTION. **CHINADOLL** *and* **RANDOLPH** *turn to watch.*

Ambassador and Mistress kiss, a sweet little kiss that gets drawn out to something more passionate and heartfelt. Then they part, giggling, still holding hands. It is a beautiful, enchanted day.

As the film unfolds, **CHINADOLL** *again addresses the audience.)*

CHINADOLL. I never knew my mother's life with the Ambassador. She would leave me and go to Beijing for days on end. As if on a secret mission. And then she would come back. I didn't even meet him until after the war. Until after she was dead. And I knew, he has to die. I will have to kill him. And that's what the beautiful girl did. *(Beat; she steals a look at the film)* She loved him, like no one she's ever loved before. And somehow, I know, I will never have a love like that. I'm not like her. Will never be like her. I'm not weak you see. I'm a communist. Don't you see? A communist?

(As **CHINADOLL** *turns back to the screen, there's a split-second moment, when* **RANDOLPH** *meets Chinadoll's eyes, when he extends his hand to hold hers. Perhaps she takes it, perhaps she doesn't. We never know for sure.*

For then **RANDOLPH** *and* **CHINADOLL** *freeze, as the film morphs into FOOTAGE of CHAIRMAN MAO addressing his band of followers – comrades with shiny, happy faces.*

As the film plays, **SIMONE** *enters, wearing a Mao suit. She holds a Little Red Book.*

On the film, the masses are chanting.

SIMONE *raises her book, and with a fervor we've not seen, joins in the chant.)*

SIMONE. Long live, Chairman Mao. Long live, Chairman Mao. Long live, Chairman Mao!

(Black out.)

End of Scene

The End

COSTUME PLOT

Act 1

Scene 1: Restaurant

CHINADOLL
Black/Purple Qipao *(calf length)*
Shoes-Black Velvet *(with purple highlights)*
Blue Overcoat *(pre-set)*
Blue Clutch Purse *(pre-set)*
Jade Bracelet
Grey Drop Earrings

RANDOLPH
Blue Pinstripe Suit
Light Blue Shirt
Black Shoes Blue
Green/Red Tie
Tan Trench Coat
Grey Fedora with Black Trim

WAITER
Simple Dark Blue Basic Male Samfoo
Black Slippers

Scene 2: Nightclub

SIMONE
Black & White Performance Dress, very showy, with Asian Feel
Black Shawl, Shear with Ostrich Feather Trim
Black Velvet High Strap Shoes
Pearl Bracelets Pearl Earrings

AMBASSADOR
Grey Tuxedo *(Dinner Jacket Style)*
Grey Pin-Stripe Pants
Grey Vest
Dark Grey Shirt
Emblem Pin on Jacket
Black Shoes

CHINESE BUSINESSMAN
Grey Suit with Vest
Dark Blue Shirt
Dark Grey Tie
Black Wingtip Shoes

Scene 3: Imperial Palace Gardens

CHINADOLL
Maroon Velvet Qipao *(ankle length)* with Clear & Black Rhinestones
Black Shoes, straps with Rhinestones
Black Beaded Clutch
Black Velvet Gloves
3-Strand Diamond Earrings
Ruby Diamond Bracelet *(left wrist)*
Diamond Ring *(right hand)*

RANDOLPH
Classic Dinner Tuxedo *(black)*
Black Shoes
Cuff Links, Studs

SERVER
Black Male Samfoo *(fancy)* with Red Embroidery of Dragon on Front
Black Slip on Shoes

Scene 4: Ambassador's Residence

SIMONE
Black & Gold Qipao, button down front *(calf length)*
White Fur Stole
Grey Rhinestone Bracelet
Grey Rhinestone Earrings
Gloves, Grey
Grey Purse
Pink Slip with Embroidery

AMBASSADOR
Grey Tuxedo Pants *(as in Scene 2)*
Grey Shirt *(as in Scene 2)*
Tie *(as in Scene 2)*
Gold, Maroon & Black Smoking Jacket
Black Shoes *(as in Scene 2)*

Scene 5: Restaurant/Imperial Palace Gardens

CHINADOLL
Same as in Scene 3

RANDOLPH
Same as in Scene 3

Scene 6: Ambassador's Residence

RANDOLPH
Same as in Scene 3
Add Overcoat
Grey Fedora with Black Trim

SIMONE
Slip from Scene 4
Black Flowered Silk Robe
Black Shoes

Scene 7: Anonymous Building Corridor

CHINADOLL
Dark Blue very simple Cotton Qipao *(calf-length)*
Flat Shoes
No Jewelry

CHINESE MAN
Tweed Jacket
Dark Blue Trench coat
Grey Shirt & Tie
Black Fedora
Black Leather Gloves
Black Wingtip Shoes

Scene 8: Interrogation Room
Grey Tuxedo Pants *(as in Scene 2)*
Grey Shirt *(as in Scene 2)*
Tie undone
Black Shoes *(as in Scene 2)*

Scene 9: Randolph's Hotel Room

CHINADOLL
Blue Velvet Qipao *(pre-set)*
Black Slip
Black Leather High Heels *(pre set)*

RANDOLPH
Red Robe
Boxers
No shirt

Scene 10: Interrogation Room

AMBASSADOR
Same as in Scene 8
Distressed Grey Shirt

Scene 11: Quiet Street

CHINADOLL
Dark Blue Trench Coat
Black Fedora
Black Wingtip Shoes
Black Leather Gloves
Black Men's Slacks

CHINESE MAN
Dark Blue Trench Coat
Black Fedora
Black Wingtip Shoes
Black Leather Gloves
Black Slacks
(Note: Chinese Man & Chinadoll's costumes for this scene should be identical)

RANDOLPH
Blue Suit Dark Blue Patterned Tie
Tan Trench Coat
Hat *(in hand)*

Act Two

Scene 11: Hospital

RANDOLPH
Boxers
Shirtless with Bandage

AMBASSADOR
Brown Suit
Tan Shirt
Tie
Overcoat
Hat

Scene 12: Restaurant

CHINADOLL
Blue Trim Qipao *(calf-length)*
Black Purse Leather *(gun inside)*
Blue Coat Dress Overcoat
Hat
Simple Black Shoes

SIMONE
Green Qipao
Brown Fur Stole
Brown Shoes

Pearl Earrings
Simple Pearl Bracelet
Gloves

WAITER
Same as in Scene 1

Scene 14: Randolph's Hotel Room

CHINADOLL
Black & Gold very sexy Qipao
Gold Strap Shoes
Gold Shear Shawl

RANDOLPH
Same as in Scene 11
Shirt unbuttoned
White Tank Undershirt

Scene 15: Alleyway

AMBASSADOR
Grey Suit Pants
Light Blue Shirt
Tie *(Loose)*
Black Shoes

CHINESE BUSINESSMAN
Grey Suit Slacks
Grey Suit Vest
Shirt
Tie
Black Shoes

Scene 16: Nightclub Dressing Room

CHINADOLL
Navy Linen Qipao
Pink Slippers

RANDOLPH
Same as in Scene 1

SIMONE
Feather Dressing Gown
Red & Black Long Slip
Red Shoes

AMBASSADOR
Grey Suit Jacket
Grey Suit Pants
Light Blue Shirt
Tie
Black Shoes

CHINESE MAN
Same as in Scene 7

Scene 17: Residence in Village Near Beijing

CHINADOLL
Same as in Scene 16
Add simple Tan Shawl

RANDOLPH
Same as in Scene 16
Add Overcoat
Add Hat

SIMONE
Mao Suit
Black Slippers

WOMAN
Mauve Kimono
Black Wig
Large Dark Shawl

PROPERTY PLOT

Onstage
2 café tables
2 chairs
2 tablecloths
2 ashtrays
Matches and striker
3 Chinese lanterns hanging

Off DSR
Small ornate table
Old film projector
Businessman's briefcase with Little Red Book inside

Wagon
Ambassador settee
Ashtray
Book
Cigarette cup with cigarettes
Empty glass
Globe bar
Misc. bottles & decanters
3 clean glasses

Off USR
Bed with hotel linens in place
Hotel table
Decanter half full
Clean glass
Ice bucket
Ashtray
Hospital Chair
Hospital bedding
Hospital table
Ashtray

Prop Shelves
Menu
Garden tray
Cigarettes in cup
3 filled flutes
Ashtray
Crystal lighter
Flute ¼ filled for Chinadoll
Opium pipe
Plate with food
Blank gun

2 other guns
Drop tray
Film canister with short piece of film inside
Tray with Simone's stage make-up

Personal Props
RANDOLPH
    Transit papers
    Cigarette box
    Handkerchief
    Money
    Letter

AMBASSADOR
    Cigarette case
    Zippo
    Money
    Envelope with cash

THE MAN
    Gloves in trench coat
    Package with film
    Garrote

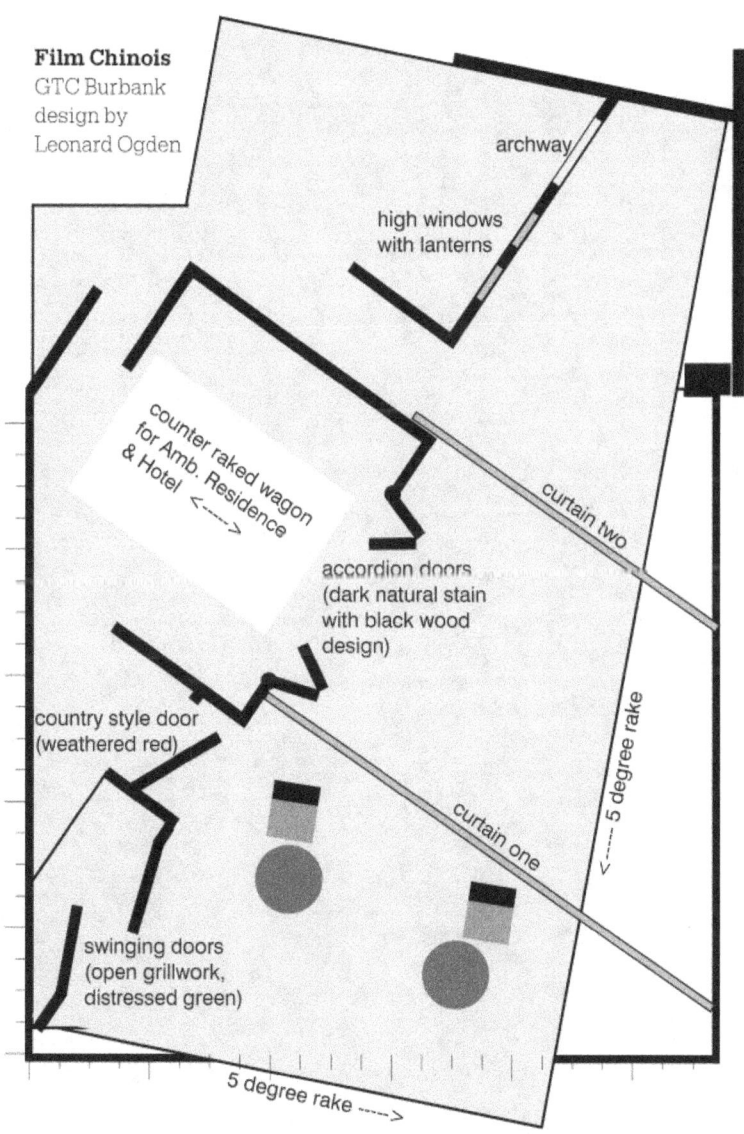

www.ingramcontent.com/pod-product-compliance
Lightning Source LLC
Chambersburg PA
CBHW070648300426
44111CB00013B/2328